DROUGHTS

BY PATRICK MERRICK

Drought!

"Drought" is from an old English word that meant "dry" or "to dry up."

As the sun rises, the sky is blue and cloudless. Today looks as if it is going to be another beautiful day. It is hard to believe that a day like this could be the start of a natural disaster. What could such a disaster be? It is a drought (DROWT).

Most other natural disasters, such as tornadoes, lightning, and hurricanes, are fast and scary. But a drought is slow. It is simply a time when there is too little rain. Droughts can last from as little as three weeks to as long as a hundred years!

This Australian lake is drying up due to lack of rain.

Necessary Rain

Rain is how the land gets the water it needs. The land needs rain so plants can grow and animals can live. Rain also fills lakes and rivers and helps stop grass fires and forest fires. People need water, too. That's because our bodies are made mostly of water!

A skeleton is all that is left of this fish after its lake home dried up.

Different Types

Droughts often go hand in hand with higher temperatures. Higher temperatures cause the ground to dry out even more.

The Sahara Desert is huge! It covers over 3.6 million square miles (9.4 million km²).

The Gobi Desert covers 500,000 square miles (1.3 million km²).

There are two kinds of droughts. One kind of drought never stops. It is called a **permanent drought**. Areas with permanent droughts are usually called **deserts**. Deserts get less than eight inches (20 cm) of rain a year. Some famous deserts are the Sahara Desert in Africa and the Gobi Desert in Asia. There are also several large deserts that can be found in the southwestern United States, such as the Mojave and the Sonoran.

The other type of drought lasts from a few weeks to a few years. It is called a **contingent drought**. Contingent droughts can happen at any time. They cause a lot of damage, because no one is ready for them. Every part of the world experiences this kind of drought. Many plants, animals, and people can die during a contingent drought.

Death Valley is a national park in California. It is part of the Mojave Desert.

Droughts Everywhere

Droughts can happen anywhere on Earth. They even happen in the United States. In 1996, there was a huge drought in the southwestern United States. The ground became so dry that fires burned over 100,000 acres (about 40,500 hectares) of trees. The farmers could not grow crops. Many cows and other animals starved because they had nothing to eat.

Droughts even affect people in big cities. In 2014, the water level in California's rivers and lakes dropped very low. People were asked not to water their lawns or take long showers. Some restaurants and flower shops had to close—there was just too little water!

"Desertification" is what happens when desert conditions spread to non-desert areas.

A bad drought is going on right now in California. Some scientists think it might be the worst drought in 500 years.

This field of corn is dying because of a drought in the United States.

Causes

El Niño and La Niña happen every three to five years.

El Niño means "little boy" in Spanish. *La Niña* means "little girl."

El Niño and La Niña each last for about one year.

Droughts are caused by many different forces—the wind, the land itself, and even the ocean. Wind carries rain clouds all over the world. If the wind does not blow rain clouds over an area, there will be no rain. Mountains sometimes make a cloud's rain fall as the cloud moves up the mountain. This can cause the other side of the mountain to have a drought.

Even though the ocean is filled with water, it is one of the biggest causes of droughts. Within the ocean there are streams of moving water called **currents**. Two of these currents are **El Niño** and **La Niña**. El Niño is a current with very warm water. La Niña is a current that is very cold. When either current comes close to land, it causes problems. Too much rain falls in some areas, causing floods. Too little rain falls in other areas, causing droughts.

Both the cold ocean currents from Antarctica and the high peaks of South America's Andes Mountains cause nearly all of the area's rain and snow to be trapped either along the coast or high up in the mountains. This means that little or no rain falls in the other parts of the region.

Drought Dangers

Between 1984 and 1985, a drought in Africa caused a famine that killed 750,000 people.

People can live for several weeks without food, but only for a few days without water.

Lack of clean water can also cause many diseases to spread.

Because everything needs water, droughts are very dangerous. Without rain, plants cannot grow. Sometimes people and animals cannot find enough food. That is called a **famine**. During a famine, people and animals become sick and even die from lack of food.

This farmer in Kenya is moving his cattle to better farmland. You can see how thin his cows are.

Stopping Droughts

The worst years of the Dust Bowl were 1934, 1936, and 1939.

During long droughts, people often permanently move to other areas. This happened during the Dust Bowl years.

Some people nicknamed the Dust Bowl years as the "Dirty Thirties."

One of the most famous droughts happened in the United States. During the 1930s, ten states went through a terrible drought. This time became known as the "Dust Bowl." Farmers lost almost all of their crops. Many of them had to sell their land and move to the city to try to find jobs and food.

The worst part of the drought was the dust storms. The wind would pick up the dry dirt and sweep it high into the air. These huge storms moved millions of tons of dirt and turned the sky as black as night. In Kansas alone, the drought and the dust storms killed 300,000 people!

This dust storm is approaching Stratford, Texas in 1935.

Droughts are hard to stop, but some things can keep them from doing as much damage. Farmers can plant trees and bushes to keep the wind from blowing the dirt around. They can also plant their crops in ways that help save the soil.

Grass fires and forest fires are big dangers during droughts.

Some crops, such as millet and sorghum, are able to tolerate droughts.

This photo shows "contour strip farming." The farmer has planted areas of corn, then short grasses to hold in the rainwater, then corn again.

Try not to pour water down the drain. Use it elsewhere, such as for watering plants in your house.

Even people in the city can help fight droughts. We can all learn to save, or **conserve**, the water we already have. Watering the grass only in the early morning or in the evening helps save water. So does shutting off the water when we are not using it. By saving water, we can help fight one of nature's worst disasters—the drought.

Only using water when you really need to is important during a drought. Be sure your sprinkler waters the grass and not the sidewalk or street, where the water is wasted.

Glossary

conserve (kon-SERV)
When you conserve something, you save it or use it carefully. It is important that we learn to conserve water.

contingent drought (con-TIN-jent DROWT)
A contingent drought is one that lasts from a few weeks to a few years.

currents (KUR-rents)
Currents are large streams of water flowing within the ocean. Currents can cause changes in our weather, including droughts.

deserts (DEZ-urts)
Deserts are areas that get very little rain. There are deserts all over the world.

El Niño (EL NEEN-yoh)
El Niño is a very warm stream of water in the ocean. Like La Niña, El Niño can cause droughts and floods when it flows close to land.

famine (FAM-in)
A famine is a time when there is too little food. Droughts can sometimes cause famines.

La Niña (LA NEEN-yuh)
La Niña is a very cold stream of water in the ocean. It can cause weather changes, including floods and droughts, when it flows near land.

permanent drought (PERM-uh-nent DROWT)
A permanent drought is one that never ends. Many deserts have permanent droughts.

To Find Out More

In the Library

Challen, Paul. *Drought and Heat Wave Alert!* New York: Crabtree, 2005.

Cunningham, Kevin. *Surviving Droughts and Famines.* Chicago: Raintree, 2012.

Marrin, Albert. *Years of Dust: The Story of the Dust Bowl.* New York: Puffin Books, 2012.

Stanley, Jerry. *Children of the Dust Bowl: The True Story of the School at Weedpatch Camp.* New York: Crown, 1992.

On the Web

Visit our Web site for links about droughts:
www.childsworld.com/links

Note to Parents, Teachers, and Librarians: We routinely check our Web links to make sure they're safe, active sites—so encourage your readers to check them out!

Index